# SAFETY FIRST!

# WATER

By Eugene Baker
Pictures by Tom Dunnington

Zachary's Workshop LTD • Creative Education

Published by Creative Education, Inc.,
123 South Broad Street, Mankato, Minnesota 56001
Copyright ©1980 by Creative Education, Inc.
International copyrights reserved in all countries.
No part of this book may be reproduced in any form without
written permission from the publisher.
Printed in the United States.

Created by "Zachary's Workshop Ltd."
Lake Forest, Illinois 60045

Library of Congress Cataloging in Publication Data
Baker, Eugene H.
    Safety first . . . water.
    SUMMARY:   Presents safety tips for swimming.
    1.  Swimming—Safety measures—Juvenile literature.
[1.  Swimming—Safety measures.   2.  Safety]
I.  Dunnington, Tom.   II.  Title.
GV838.52.B34     797.2'1'0289     79-26951     ISBN 0-87191-740-8

Rover          Basil

"Hey Rover," yelled Basil. "Watch this dive."

"I'll make a bigger splash than you do," answered Rover.

Can you see
what's wrong?

5

- Do not dive in strange water.
- Be aware of sharp objects in water.
- Do not swim under a pier.
- Do not run on a slippery pier.

"Let's swim way out and watch the birds," said Basil.

"I'll stay here. I like to run into the waves," answered Rover.

# Can you see what's wrong?

- Do not swim in unsupervised moving water.
- Watch for dangerous animal life in the water.
- Do not swim long distances alone.
- Stay out of water after eating.
- Watch for sharp objects in sand.

11

"This is fun!" called Basil. "I'll race you to the end of the pool."

"I'll beat you," answered Rover. "Watch my new kick."

Can you see what's wrong?

- Swim safe distance from diving board.
- Do not talk to lifeguard.
- No glass or bottles in pool area.
- Do not run on pool deck.
- Do not push people into pool.

15

"I practice after each lesson,"
said Basil.

"How do I keep my face out of
the water?" asked Rover. "The water
hurts my eyes."

Can you see what's wrong?

16

- Learn to swim to survive.
- Know how to use life saving equipment.
- Know what to do in an emergency.

"I'm hot!" says Basil. "I'm going to take a swim."

"I'm going to eat some more," says Rover. "It may be a long time before supper."

Can you see what's wrong?

21

- Never swim alone.
- Swim only in supervised areas.
- Do not dive in unknown water.
- Stay out of water in a storm.
- Never eat a heavy meal before swimming.

NO SWIMMING

"Throw out the inner tube," said Basil.
"I'll dive in and come up inside."
"Want to race across the lake?"
asked Rover.

Can you see what's wrong?

- Do not run on slippery raft.
- Do not use inflated inner tube or raft for swimming ability.
- Do not push anyone into the water.

# REMEMBER NOW. . . . .

Do not dive in strange water.

Be aware of sharp objects in water.

Do not swim under a pier.

Do not run on a slippery pier.

———————————

Do not swim in unsupervised moving water.

Watch for dangerous animal life in the water.

Do not swim long distances alone.

Stay out of water after eating.

Watch for sharp objects in sand.

Swim safe distance from
  diving board.
Do not talk to lifeguard.
No glass or bottles in pool area.
Do not run on pool deck.
Do not push people into pool.

———————————

Learn to swim to survive.
Know how to use life saving
  equipment.
Know what to do in an
  emergency.

Never swim alone.

Swim only in supervised areas.

Do not dive in unknown water.

Stay out of water in a storm.

Never eat a heavy meal
before swimming.

_____

Do not run on slippery raft.

Do not use inflated inner tube or
raft for swimming ability.

Do not push anyone into the
water.

EUGENE BAKER is Vice-President for Curriculum and Materials Development, Zachary's Workshop Ltd., Lake Forest, Illinois. Dr. Baker graduated from Carthage College, Carthage, Illinois. He received his M.A. and Ph.D. in education from Northwestern University. He has worked as a teacher, as a principal, and as director of curriculum and instruction.

Gene is the author of many children's books, educational audio-visual materials, and numerous articles on reading, guidance, and learning research. One of his best-known series is the *I Want to Be* books. In addition to writing and speaking widely, he has served as consultant on various educational programs at both national and local levels. Dr. Baker also teaches Adult Sunday Church School.

Dr. Baker's practical help to schools where new programs are evolving is sparked by his boundless enthusiasm. He likes to see reading, social studies, and language arts taught with countless resources, including many books, to encourage students to think independently, creatively, and critically. Gene and his wife, Donna, live in Arlington Heights, Illinois. They have a son and two daughters.